811	Grimes, Nikki.	
Gri		
C.l	Meet Danitra Brown	

BC# 30488000015045 $10.15

DATE DUE	BORROWER'S NAME	ROOM NUMBER
9-25-00	Jasmine Brown	304
March 21/02	Teshia Mattox	207
	Ashonte Hall	205

MEET DANITRA BROWN

NIKKI GRIMES

ILLUSTRATED BY FLOYD COOPER

MEET DANITRA BROWN

NIKKI GRIMES
ILLUSTRATED BY
FLOYD COOPER

A MULBERRY PAPERBACK BOOK · NEW YORK

The Library of Congress has cataloged the Lothrop, Lee & Shepard
edition of Meet Danitra Brown as follows:
Grimes, Nikki. Meet Danitra Brown / by Nikki Grimes ;
illustrated by Floyd Cooper.
p. cm.
ISBN 0-688-12073-3.—ISBN 0-688-12074-1 (lib. bdg.)
1. Afro-American—Juvenile poetry. 2. Children's poetry, American.
[1. Afro-Americans—Poetry. 2. City and town life—Poetry.
3. Friendship—Poetry. 4. Single-parent family—Poetry. 5. American
poetry.] I. Cooper, Floyd, ill. II. Title. PS3557.R489982M44
1995 811'.54—dc20 92-43707 CIP AC

1 3 5 7 9 10 8 6 4 2
First Mulberry Edition, 1997
ISBN 0-688-15471-9

For my sister Carol,
an original character if ever there was one,
and for Debra Jackson-Whyte,
who taught me a thing or two about friendship
—N.G.

For Erica
—F.C.

You Oughta Meet Danitra Brown

You oughta meet Danitra Brown,
the most splendiferous girl in town.
I oughta know, 'cause she's my friend.

She's not afraid to take a dare.
If something's hard, she doesn't care.
She'll try her best, no matter what.

She doesn't mind what people say.
She always does things her own way.
Her spirit's old, my mom once said.

I only know I like her best
'cause she sticks out from all the rest.
She's only she—Danitra Brown.

Jump Rope Rhyme

Zuri Jackson. That's my name.
Count to three, it's still the same.
Turn the rope and watch me spin.
Quick, Danitra! Jump on in!

Coke-bottle Brown

Dumb old Freddy Watson called my friend "Coke-bottle Brown."
(So what if her bifocals are big and thick and round?)
"Pay him no never mind, Zuri," is what Danitra said,
then hands on hips, she turned away and lifted up her head.

"Me, Danitra Brown, I've got no time for Freddy's mess.
Let him call me silly names, 'cause I could not care less.
Can't waste time on some boy who thinks it's funny bein' mean.
Got books to read and hills to climb that Freddy's never seen."

Then dumb old Freddy Watson called me "toothpick legs" and spit.
I stared him down, and balled my fists and said, "Okay! That's it!"
But suddenly I thought about the words Danitra said.
I rolled my eyes and grabbed my books and turned away instead.

Purple

Once you've met my friend Danitra, you can spot her miles away.
She's the only girl around here who wears purple every day.
Whether summer's almost over or spring rains are pouring down,
if you see a girl in purple, it must be Danitra Brown.

Purple socks and jeans and sneakers, purple ribbons for her hair.
Purple shirts and slacks and sweaters, even purple underwear!
Purple dresses, shorts, and sandals, purple coat and purple gloves.
There's just no mistake about it: Purple's what Danitra loves!

Purple is okay, I guess. I have worn it once or twice.
But there's nothing wrong with yellow. Red and blue are also nice.
So one day I asked Danitra if once in a while, for fun,
She would wear another color, just to surprise everyone.

But her mom has told her stories about queens in Timbuktu.
And it seems they all wore purple—never red or green or blue.
Now, she might just be a princess. After all, who's to say?
So just in case, she'll dress in purple each and every day!

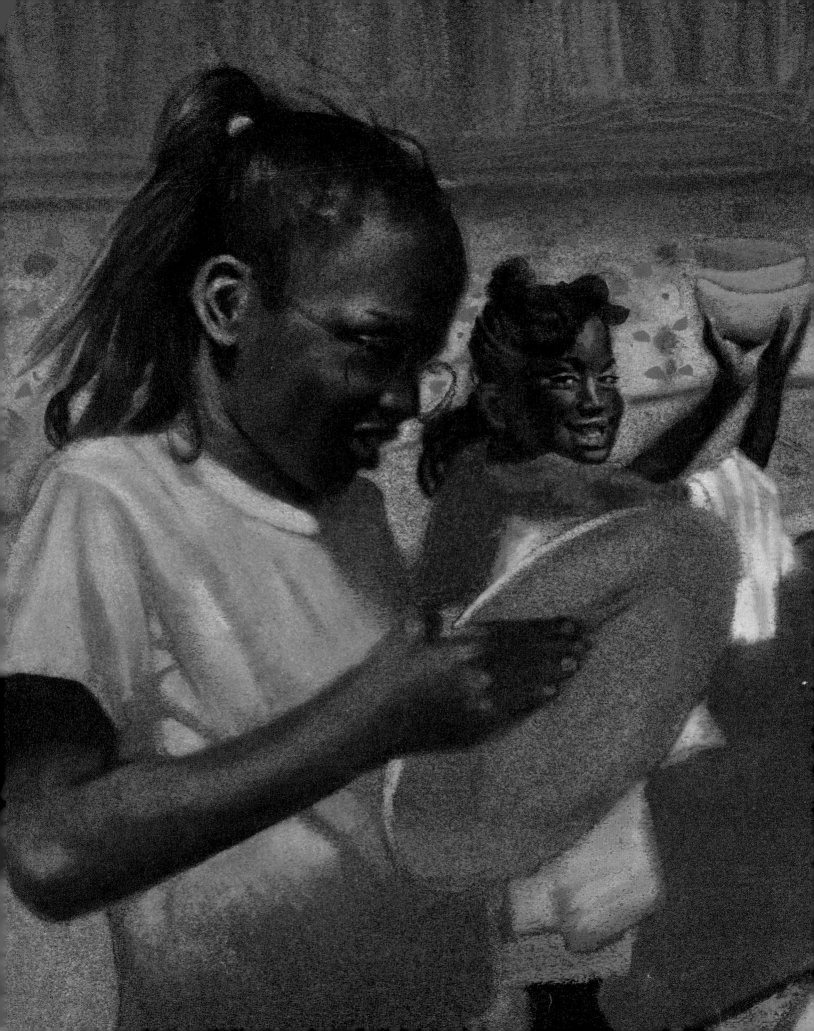

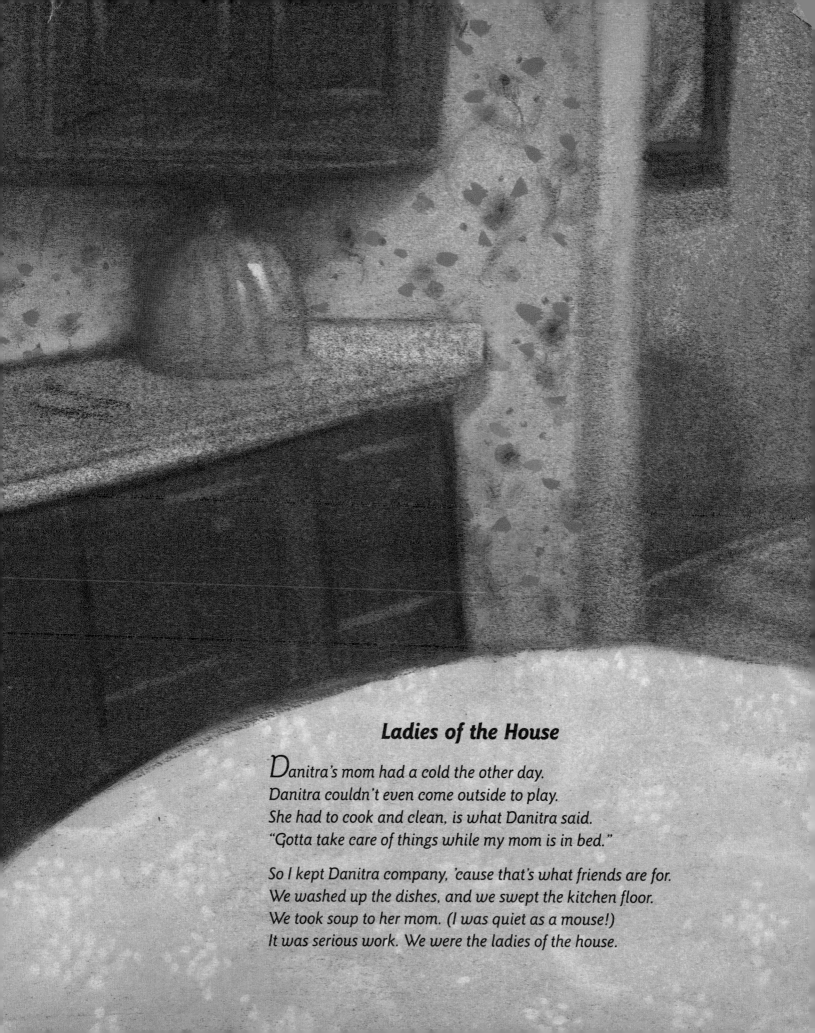

Ladies of the House

Danitra's mom had a cold the other day.
Danitra couldn't even come outside to play.
She had to cook and clean, is what Danitra said.
"Gotta take care of things while my mom is in bed."

So I kept Danitra company, 'cause that's what friends are for.
We washed up the dishes, and we swept the kitchen floor.
We took soup to her mom. (I was quiet as a mouse!)
It was serious work. We were the ladies of the house.

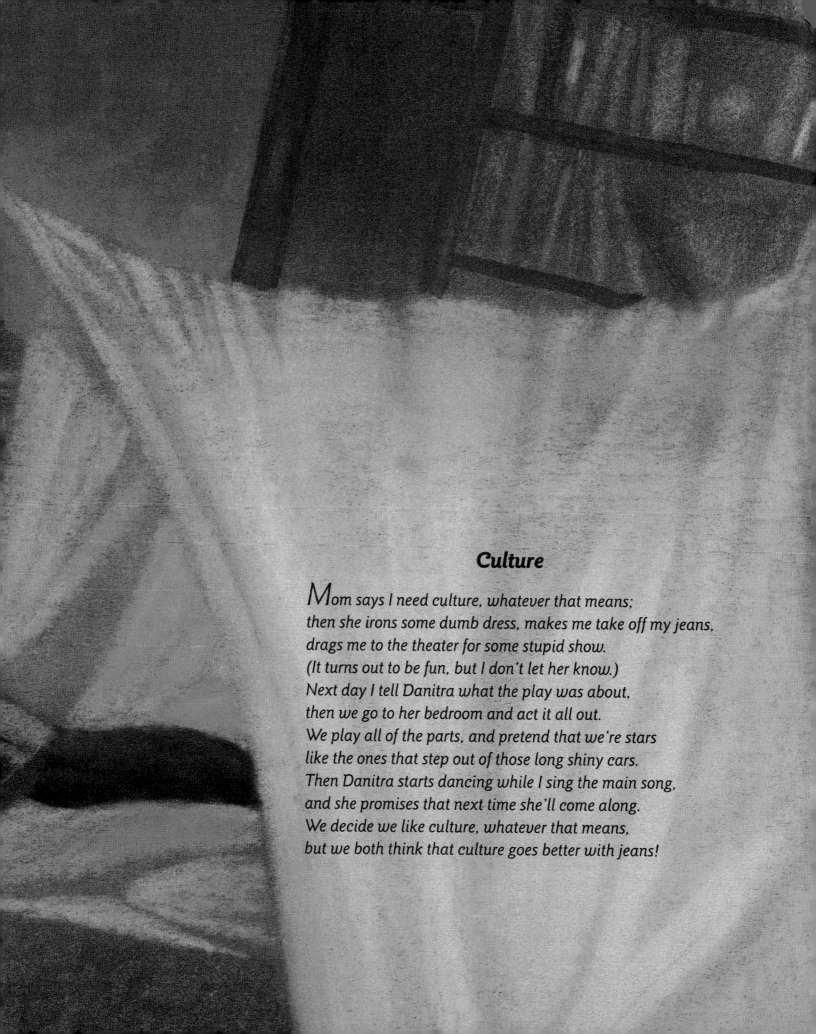

Culture

Mom says I need culture, whatever that means;
then she irons some dumb dress, makes me take off my jeans,
drags me to the theater for some stupid show.
(It turns out to be fun, but I don't let her know.)
Next day I tell Danitra what the play was about,
then we go to her bedroom and act it all out.
We play all of the parts, and pretend that we're stars
like the ones that step out of those long shiny cars.
Then Danitra starts dancing while I sing the main song,
and she promises that next time she'll come along.
We decide we like culture, whatever that means,
but we both think that culture goes better with jeans!

Mom and Me Only

Some kids at school have a mom and a dad.
I've got Mom and me only.
On Parents' Night it makes me mad
that it's Mom and me only.
"You've got it good," Danitra says when I am sad.
"Your mama loves you twice as much. Is that so bad?"
Danitra knows just what to say to make me glad.
With her around, I'm never lonely.

Sweet Blackberry

Danitra says my skin's like double chocolate fudge
'cause I'm so dark.
The kids at school say it another way.
"You so black, girl," they say,
"at night, people might think
you ain't nothin' but a piece o' sky."

I never cry, but inside there's a hurting place.
I make sure no one sees it on my face.
Then mama tells me, "Next time, honey, you just say,
The blacker the berry, the sweeter the juice."

Now that's just what I do.
I sure wish I had told them that before.
Those kids don't bother teasin' me no more.

The Secret

Danitra's scared of pigeons. I promised not to tell,
then I opened my big mouth and out the secret fell.
I tried to shove it right back in, though it was much too late.
I told her I was sorry, but Danitra didn't wait.
"What kind of friend are you?" she yelled before she stomped away.
She wouldn't hardly say a word to me the whole next day.
She finally forgave me, but not until I swore
to never, ever give away a secret anymore.

Summertime Sharing

Danitra sits hunched on the stoop and pouts.
I ask her what there is to pout about.
"Nothin' much," she says to me,
but then I see her eyes following the ice cream man.

I shove my hand into my pocket
and find the change there where I left it.
"Be right back," I yell, running down the street.
Me and my fast feet are there and back in just two shakes.

Danitra breaks the Popsicle in two and gives me half.
The purple ice trickles down her chin. I start to laugh.
Her teeth flash in one humongous grin,
telling me she's glad that I'm her friend without even saying a word.

Bike Crazy

Watch me and Danitra biking down the street,
wheee! round the corner. There go Danitra's feet
right off the pedals, arms thrown up to the sky.
Me, I laugh and yell out, "Fly, Danitra! Fly!"

Stories to Tell

Danitra says she's gonna win the Nobel Prize,
and I can tell by looking in her eyes
how much she means it.

I see her writing rhymes and stories in a book.
She slips a page to me and lets me look,
like it's our secret.

She writes about our friends, our neighborhood, and me,
the places that we'll go and what we'll be
when we all grow up.

Some teachers say Danitra's rhymes are wrong
because some of her lines are extra long.
I think they're perfect.

If Danitra says she's gonna win the Nobel Prize,
I double-dare anyone to roll his eyes.
I know she'll do it!

New Beginnings

*A new girl moved in down the street. I said hello,
and told her that she smiled like someone I know.
I told her that she oughta meet Danitra Brown,
the greatest, most splendiferous girl in town.*

NIKKI GRIMES

most frequently describes herself as an artist rather than a writer, with interests ranging from music and theater to photography and handcrafts. Nikki is the author of more than a dozen books for children and calls writing her first love and poetry her greatest pleasure. She lives in San Pedro, California.

FLOYD COOPER

can't remember when he didn't love to draw. "My earliest recollection," he says, "was getting a piece of Sheetrock and drawing this nice, big, sprawling picture of a duck on the side of our house." Floyd went on to study art on full scholarship at the University of Oklahoma. After graduating he worked as a freelance commercial artist before he illustrated his first children's book in 1988. Floyd makes his home in Parlin, New Jersey.